AF225874

The Reading Nature Guide
to the
DEADLY SNAKES
of
SOUTH AFRICA
by
Johan Hefer

REANING NATURE GUIDE TO THE DEADLY SNAKES OF
SOUTH AFRICA by Johan Hefer

Series: Reading Nature

Published by: Johannis Antonius Publishers (Pty) Ltd

PO Box 53, Mooi River, 3300, South Africa

© Johannis Antonius Publishers

All rights reserved

Photos by:

Nick Evans, Luke Kemp, Johan Hefer, Chad Keates, Tyrone
Ping, Barbara Louw, Tawnee Funston

Series Publisher: Johan Hefer

Series Educational Expert: Lorna Bruwer

ISBN:

PDF eBook: 978-1-928421-00-9

Kindle eBook: 978-1-928421-04-7

Paperback: 978-1-928421-02-3

South Africa is blessed with some of the best *biodiversity* in the world. Included in this biodiversity is some of the most deadly snakes in the world.

If you are bitten by a snake you should seek medical attention. It will also help if you can describe the snake you were bitten by.

All words in *italics* are explained in a glossary at the end of this book.

Puff Adder

Bitis arietans

Habitat	Common throughout Southern Africa.
Habits	Slow moving, bad tempered. Hisses and puffs when disturbed.
Enemies	Other snakes and birds of prey
Prey	Rats, mice, lizards and toads.
Reproduction	*Livebearer* giving birth to 20-40 babies.
Danger	Extremely dangerous bites are frequent.
Venom	Potent *cytotoxic* venom leading to extreme pain and swelling. Death in 24 hours if untreated.
Size	Average 90 centimetres Maximum 1.7 metres

The puff adder is one of the most dangerous snakes in Africa. It uses *camouflage* to blend into its surroundings.

It is an *ambush hunter* waiting for days or even weeks for prey to come past.

The colours of the puff adder can be very varied based on its location.

Gaboon Adder

Bitis gabonica

Habitat	Thickly wooded lowland *forests* in Kwa-Zulu Natal.
Habits	Sluggish and tend to stay in one place for long times. Very shy and placid nature.
Enemies	Man.
Prey	Rats, hares, toads and ground birds.
Reproduction	*Livebearer* giving birth to 16-30 babies.
Danger	Very potent venom with the longest fangs of any snake. Very few bites due to the snake's shyness.
Venom	Potent *cytotoxic* venom leading to extreme pain and swelling. Also delivers a very large quantity of venom.
Size	Average 1 metre Maximum 1.8 metres

The gaboon adder is a very shy snake and only lives in a small part of Kwa-Zulu Natal. They also occur in large parts of Tropical Africa.

The gaboon adder is the biggest viper species in the world and have the longest fangs of any venomous snake in the world.

They are masters of *camouflage* and hunt by ambushing their prey.

Gaboon adders are beautiful snakes and need our protection.

Black Mamba

Dendroaspis polylepis

Habitat	Moist *savanna* and lowland *forests,* in trees and on the ground.
Habits	Very alert and unpredictable snake.
Enemies	Birds of prey and other snakes. Fully grown adults have very few enemies.
Prey	Rats and mice, dassies and other small mammals.
Reproduction	Lays 6-17 eggs in summer.
Danger	One of the deadliest snakes in the world.
Venom	Very potent *neurotoxic* venom leading to paralysis. Death in 6-15 hours if untreated.
Size	Average 3 metres Maximum 4.5 metres

The black mamba is one of the most feared snakes in the world. A bite from this snake that is not treated will lead to death.

Black mambas like most snakes are very shy and would rather run away than bite. Like cobras they can make a hood if they feel scared.

The black mamba gets its name from the black inside of its mouth and not its colour. These snakes are very long and can reach 4.5m!

Green Mamba

Dendroaspis angusticeps

Habitat	Evergreen lowland *forest* and moist *savanna*.
Habits	Tree-living species that is seldom seen on the ground. Very graceful but shy and not aggressive.
Enemies	Other snakes.
Prey	Birds, bird eggs and small tree-living mammals.
Reproduction	Lays 6-17 eggs in summer.
Danger	Although it has potent venom it is shy and avoids humans.
Venom	Dangerous *neurotoxic* venom which will require medical attention.
Size	Average 1.8 metres Maximum 2.5 metres

The green mamba is closely related to the black mamba. This is a very shy snake and is seldom seen. They live in trees where they spend most of their time.

They are still very dangerous snakes and someone that has been bitten requires immediate medical attention.

Other harmless green snakes are often mistaken for the green mamba like the spotted bush snake below.

Twig snake

Thelotornis capensis

Habitat	Trees and shrubs in moist *savanna* and lowland *forests*.
Habits	Mostly lives in low shrubs, bushes and trees. Timid and retiring snake.
Enemies	Birds of prey and other snakes.
Prey	Chameleons and other tree living lizards.
Reproduction	Lays 4-18 eggs in summer.
Danger	Dangerous venom but due to the shyness of the snake bites are rare.
Venom	Dangerous *hemotoxic* venom.
Size	Average 1 metres Maximum 1.6 metres

The twig snake is one of the shyest snakes. It hides in bushes, blending into the surroundings perfectly.

The snake will sit there until prey comes by. It will then strike like a flash.

If it feels scared it will inflate its neck like in the picture above, to try and look larger. These snakes seldom bite but have a very dangerous venom.

Boomslang

Dispholidus typus

Habitat	Trees and shrubs in arid and moist *savanna*, lowland *forest* and *fynbos*.
Habits	Shy snake that mostly stays in trees and shrubs. Hunts its prey during the day
Enemies	Birds of prey and other snakes.
Prey	Chameleons and lizards, birds and eggs.
Reproduction	Lays 8-14 eggs in late spring to mid-summer.
Danger	Deadly venom but due to its shy nature, bites are rare.
Venom	Dangerous *hemotoxic* venom.
Size	Average 1.8 metres Maximum 2.5 metres

The boomslang has one of the most dangerous venoms in the world but due to its shy nature bites are rare.

The snake stays in trees and shrubs and hunts from there. They have very big eyes.

Males tend to be green in colour while females tend to be brown. Young snakes are brown with white under their lip and very green eyes.

Cape Cobra

Naja nivea

Habitat	*Fynbos*, *Karoo* and arid *savanna*
Habits	Active during the day. Very aggressive and will strike easily.
Enemies	Birds of prey and other snakes.
Prey	Rodents, birds, other snakes, lizards and toads.
Reproduction	Lays 8-20 eggs in mid-summer.
Danger	Extremely dangerous cobra whose bites are common and often fatal.
Venom	Dangerous *neurotoxic* venom.
Size	Average 1.2 metres Maximum 2 metres

The cape cobra is responsible for the most human fatalities in South Africa. A highly toxic venom combined with an aggressive defensive response to threats means that bites are frequent and very serious.

The cape cobra has a wide variety of colour forms.

The snake is known for climbing into trees full of nesting birds to prey on the hatchlings.

Forest Cobra

Naja melanoleuca

Habitat	Lowland *forest* and moist *savanna*.
Habits	An active and alert cobra of the forest. Very comfortable in both the trees and in water.
Enemies	Other snakes.
Prey	Toads, frogs, small mammals, birds and snakes.
Reproduction	Lays 11-26 eggs in summer.
Danger	Extremely venomous but due to its shy nature bites are rare.
Venom	Highly *neurotoxic* venom.
Size	Average 1.5 metres Maximum 2.7 metres

The forest cobra is a shy snake that does not often come into contact with man.

It does however have a serious bite and is the longest cobra in Africa.

The forest cobra is known to even feed on fish at times.

Like most snakes the forest cobra is very agile and climbs trees very quickly.

Snouted Cobra

Naja annuiifera

Habitat	Arid and moist *savanna*.
Habits	Typically active at night. Not aggressive but will stand its ground until it can flee.
Enemies	Birds of prey and other snakes.
Prey	Toads, rodents, birds and their eggs, lizards and other snakes.
Reproduction	Lays 8-33 eggs in early summer.
Danger	Large cobra with a serious bite.
Venom	Potent *neurotoxic* venom.
Size	Average 1.2 metres Maximum 3 metres

The snouted cobra is one of Africa's largest cobras. It is not an aggressive snake but will stand its ground if it is confronted until it can flee.

This snake normally looks for food during the night and therefore bites often occur on the lower leg during the night.

Mozambique Spitting Cobra

Naja mossambica

Habitat	Moist *savanna* and lowland *forest*.
Habits	More active at night but will bask in the day. Shy snake that will spit if threatened. Often found in homes looking for food.
Enemies	Other snakes.
Prey	Toads, small mammals, birds, lizards and snakes.
Reproduction	Lays 10-22 eggs in mid-summer.
Danger	Potent venom and spits venom into the eyes.
Venom	Predominantly *cytotoxic* causing tissue damage.
Size	Average 1 metres Maximum 1.5 metres

This is a spitting cobra that project venom into the eyes if it feels threatened.

It also frequently comes into contact with humans and therefore is one of the more dangerous snakes in its area.

Black Spitting Cobra

Naja nigricollis woodi

Habitat	Mountains and rocky outcrops.
Habits	Rare snake that spits venom.
Enemies	Other snakes.
Prey	Snakes, lizards, toads and small mammals.
Reproduction	Lays 10-20 eggs.
Danger	Potent venom and spits venom into the eyes but is seldom seen.
Venom	Predominantly *cytotoxic* causing tissue damage.
Size	Average 1.2 metres Maximum 2 metres

This is one of the rarest snakes and is seldom encountered by man. It is listed as rare.

This cobra will also spit venom into your eyes if it feels scared.

Rinkhals

Hemachatus haemachatus

Habitat	Grassland, moist *savanna*, lowland *forest* and *fynbos*.
Habits	Common throughout its range and often found close to human habitation.
Enemies	Birds of prey and other snakes.
Prey	Mostly toads but also lizards, rodents, snakes and birds and their eggs.
Reproduction	Gives birth to 20-30 young in late summer.
Danger	Although venom is deadly human fatalities are rare. Also spits venom.
Venom	Dangerous *neurotoxic venom*.
Size	Average 1 metres Maximum 1.5 metres

This is one of the most frequently encountered snakes. It is often found close to human habitation in its range.

It spits venom if it feels threatened. It may also try to play dead as can be seen in the above photo. Do not pick it up if it is playing dead!

Biodiversity: The variety of living things in a given place—whether a small stream, an extensive desert, all the forests in the world, the oceans, or the entire planet—is called its *biodiversity*, which is short for biological diversity.

Some snakes give birth to live young and some snakes lay eggs.

- **Livebearers** (also known as ovoviviparous) give birth to live baby snakes.

- **Oviparous** snakes lay eggs that hatch later similar to chickens.

Venomous snakes in South Africa has venom that falls broadly into three categories:

- **Cytotoxic** venom which affects the muscles and other materials the body is made up of. It literally destroys the cells of the affected area.

- **Neurotoxic** venom affects the brain and spinal cord leading to the heart and lungs stopping to function.

- **Hemotoxic** venom destroys the red bloods cells which leads to uncontrollable bleeding both internally and externally.

Camouflage a way of hiding by colouring and patterns so that it looks like its surroundings.

Ambush hunter: A snake lies waiting for prey using camouflage until prey gets close enough to catch.

Forest is land that is covered with trees and shrubs.

Savanna is a grassland containing scattered trees.

Fynbos is an area mostly in the western cape containing endemic species like proteas and bulbous plants in the winter rainfall area.

Karoo is an area mostly in the Western, Norther and Eastern Cape which is semi-desert.